HOW TO DRAW
ALL THE THINGS
for kids

ALLI KOCH

this book
BELONGS TO

_____

LET'S DRAW!

The nice thing about being an artist is that you make the rules. Everyone has their own style, which is why your drawings will look different than someone else's. In this book, each thing is broken down into steps. My goal is to help you see the simple parts of what may seem like a hard thing to draw.

We will start with the most basic outline and work our way up. You will start to see a pattern with each thing we draw; starting with simple guide lines, then breaking down "C" and "S" shaped lines, and lastly erasing the unneeded lines for the finished look. Don't forget to draw your lines lightly first so that it is easier to erase them. My favorite thing to say when drawing is:

If it was perfect, it would not look handmade!

I cannot wait for you to get started.
Happy drawing!

TOOLS

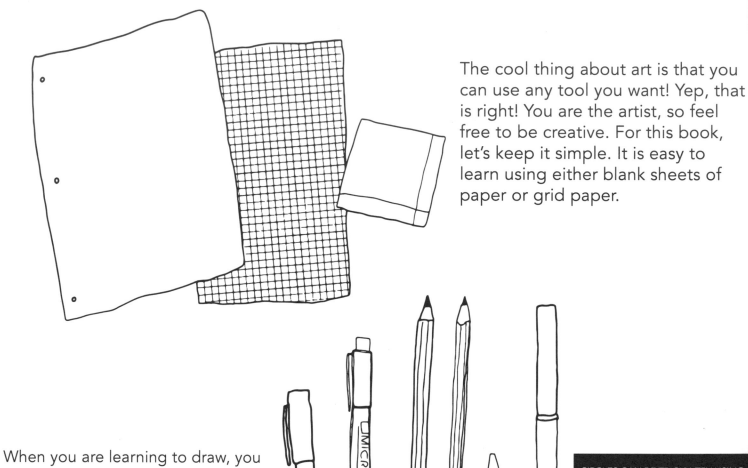

The cool thing about art is that you can use any tool you want! Yep, that is right! You are the artist, so feel free to be creative. For this book, let's keep it simple. It is easy to learn using either blank sheets of paper or grid paper.

When you are learning to draw, you really only need a pencil and a good eraser. To follow the step-by-step instructions in this book, draw everything lightly, then go over your lines with whatever tool you would like to use. You could use different pens, markers, colored pencils, or even crayons.

CIRCLES CAN BE TRICKY. TRY USING A PENNY OR CIRCLE STENCIL TO HELP!

BREAK IT DOWN

Anyone can draw! If you can write your ABCs (which I am pretty sure you can do!), then you can draw everything in this book. Each thing can be broken down into either straight lines, or "C" and "S" shaped lines. Almost anything you see that is round is simply two "C" shaped lines put together. An "S" shaped line is used when something has a dip or curvy line.

Remember, if you see thin or gray lines in this book, draw those lines lightly since you will either be erasing them or going over them with a thicker line.

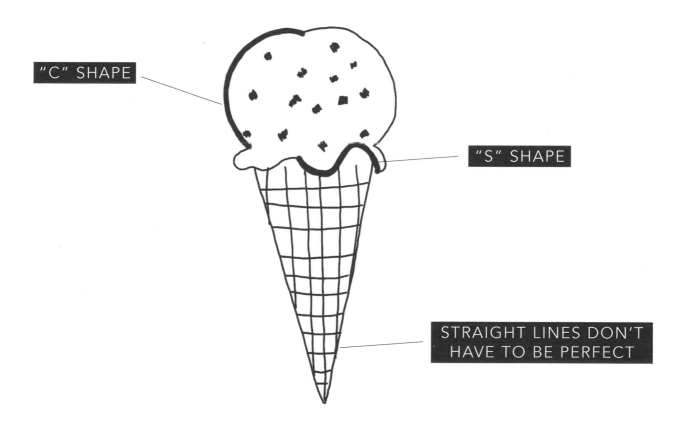

"C" SHAPE

"S" SHAPE

STRAIGHT LINES DON'T HAVE TO BE PERFECT

ICE CREAM

How many licks does it take to finish a single scoop of ice cream? About 50!

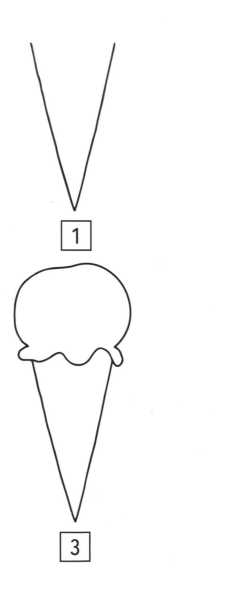

1

3

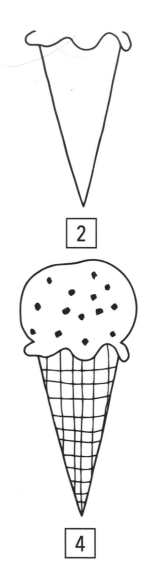

2

4

1

2

3

4

FRUIT

Strawberries are the only fruit with seeds on the outside.

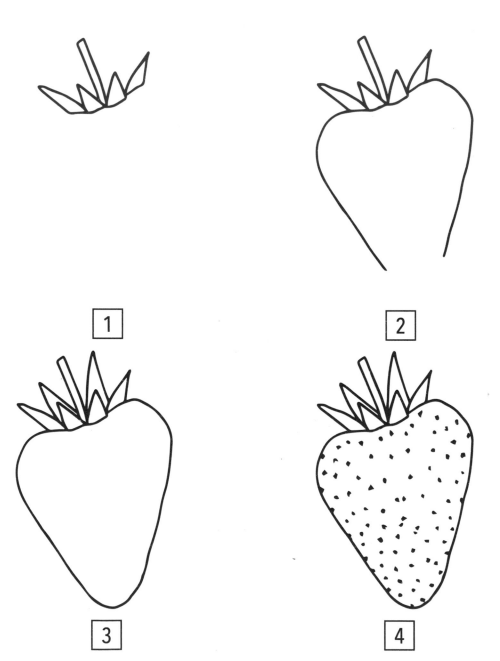

If the bottom of a pineapple smells sweet, then you know it is ready to eat.

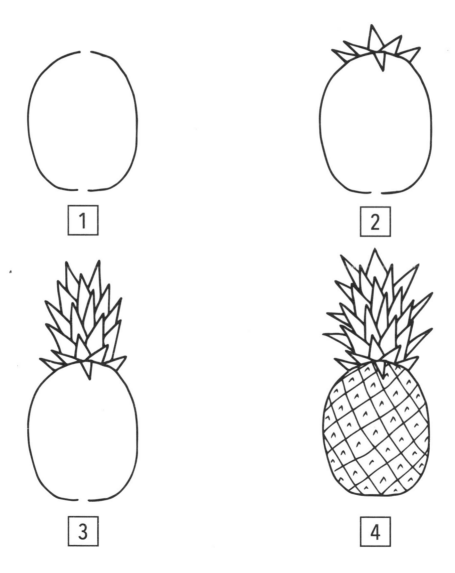

CUPCAKE

The largest cupcake ever made was 3 feet tall and weighed 2,594 pounds.

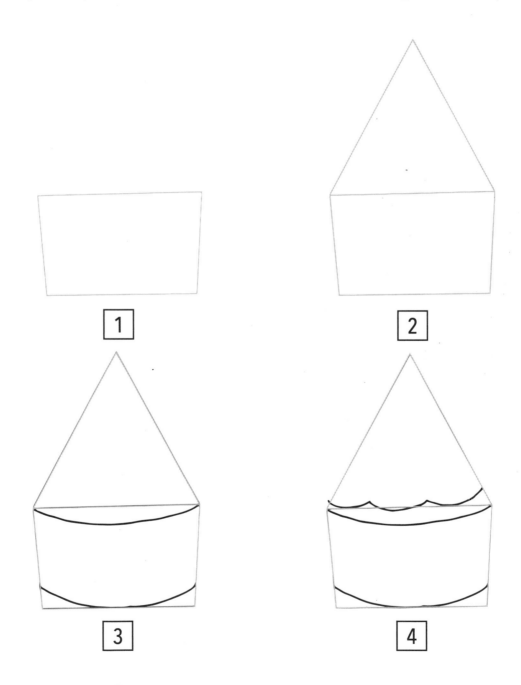

5

6

7

8

MAKEUP

In Morrisville, PA, you need a permit to wear makeup. Thankfully no one enforces this law!

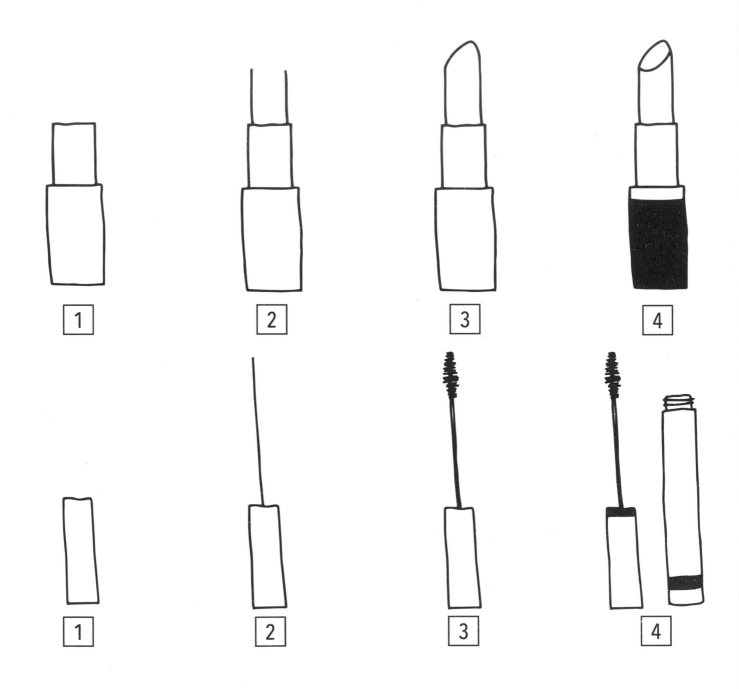

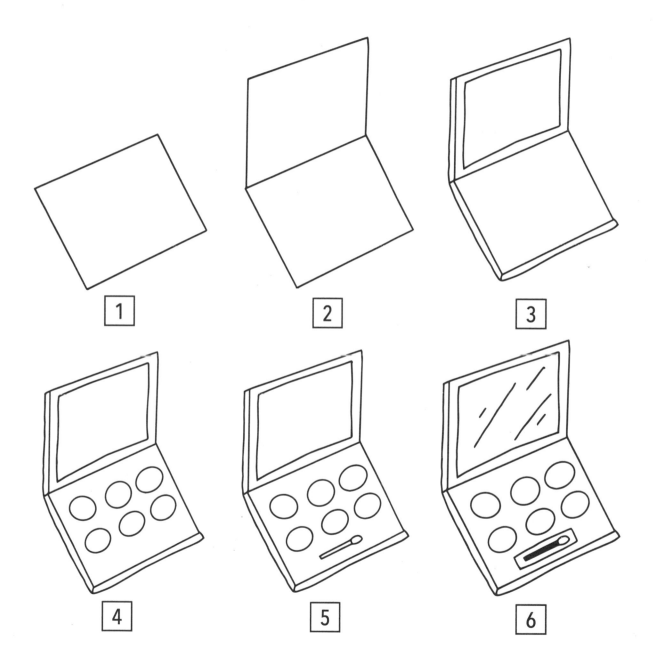

1

2

3

4

5

6

HATS

The first baseball cap was made of straw.

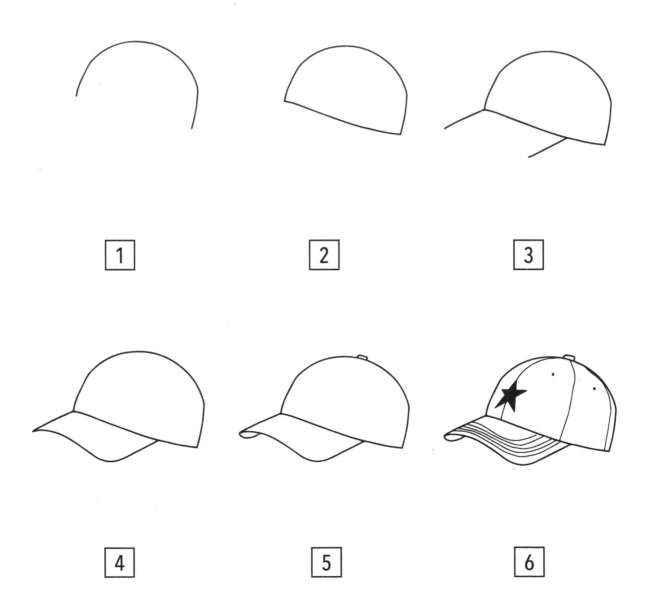

Back in the day, the different bends of a cowboy hat indicated where someone was from.

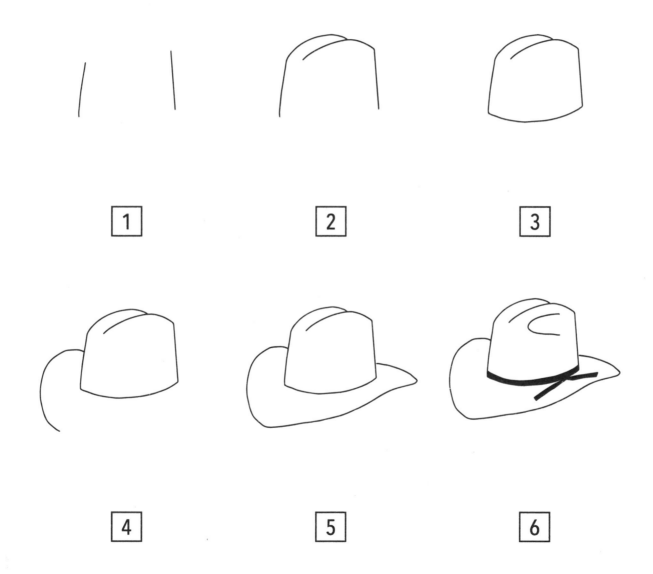

1

2

3

4

5

6

SHOES

A ballet slipper can be worn on the left or right foot.

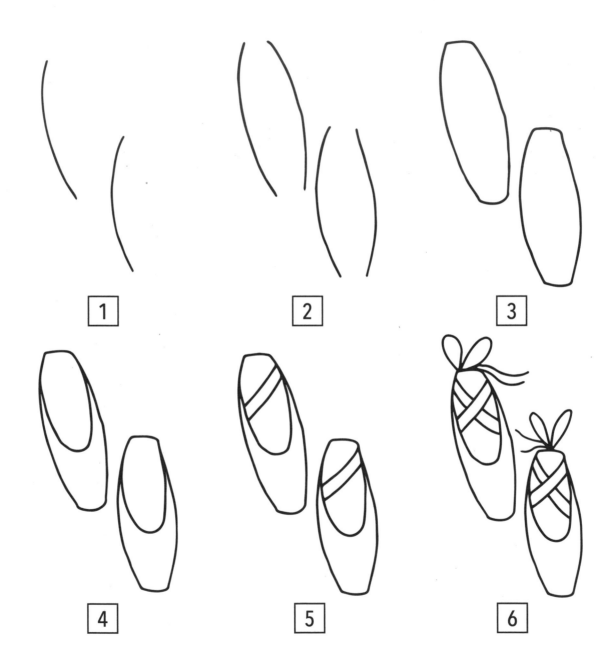

There is no rule that a soccer player must wear cleats, only that they must have shoes on.

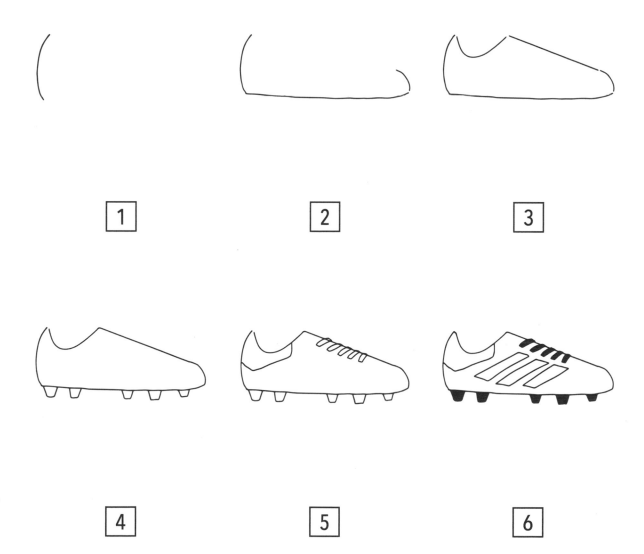

1

2

3

4

5

6

CAMERA

Trillions of photos are taken around the world each year.

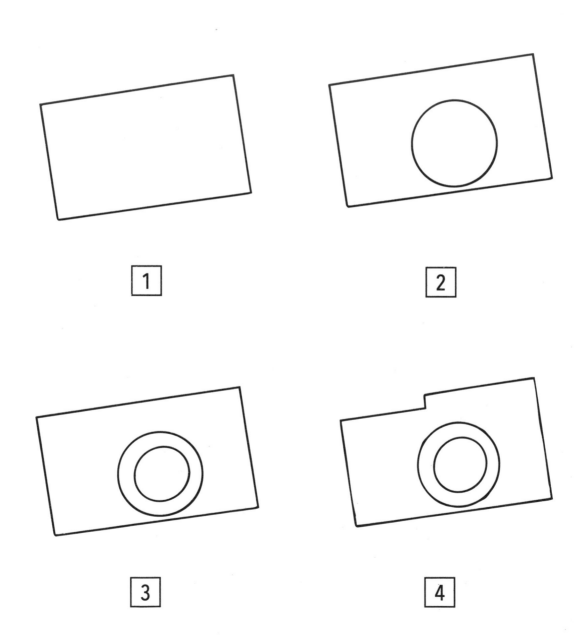

1

2

3

4

5

6

7

8

MUSIC THINGS

Sound travels in waves.

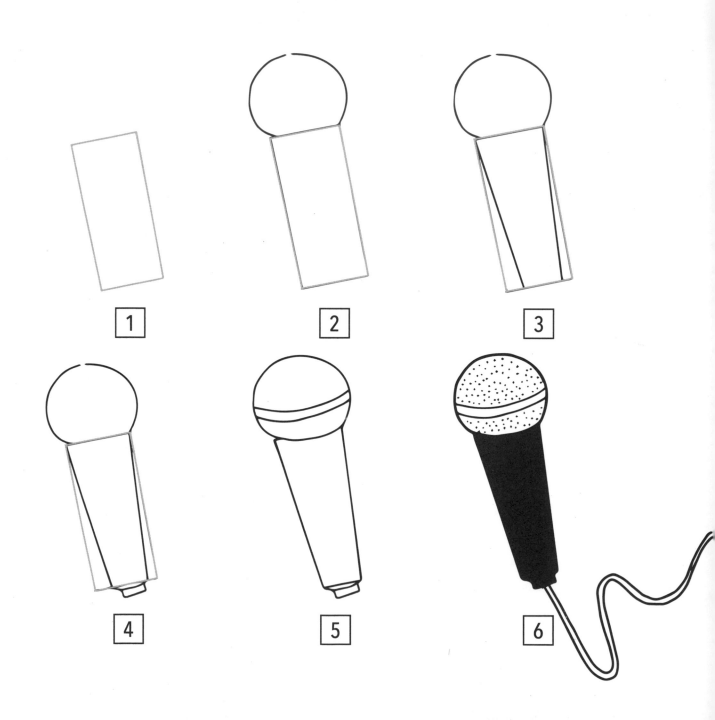

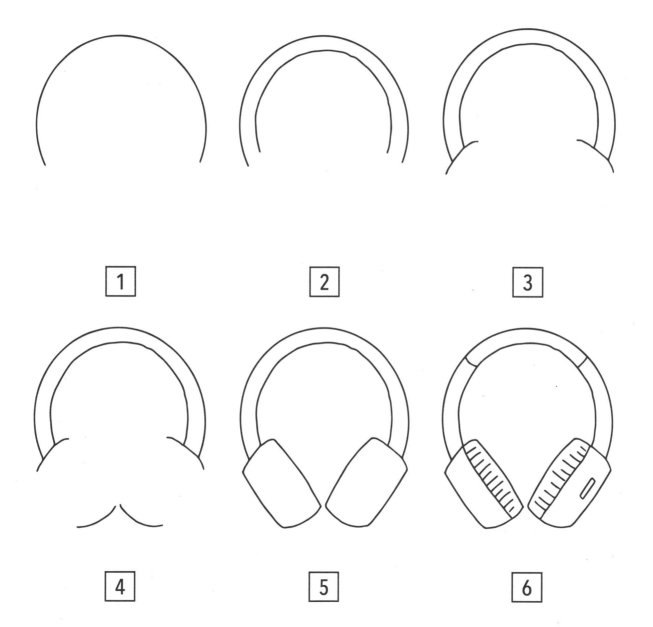

1

2

3

4

5

6

ART THINGS

The human eye can see green better than any other color.

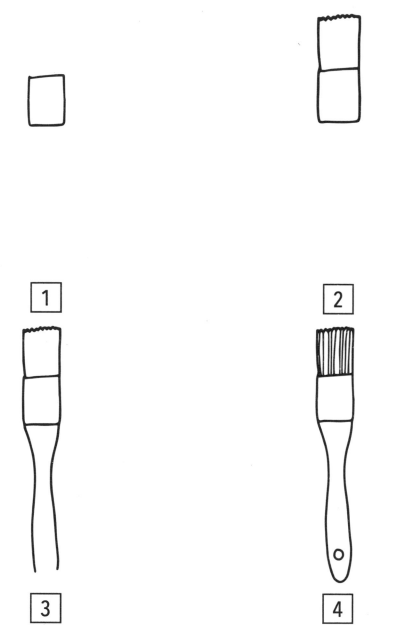

1

2

3

4

TRUCK

Trucks haul more than half of all the goods we use in the United States.

1

2

3

4

5

6

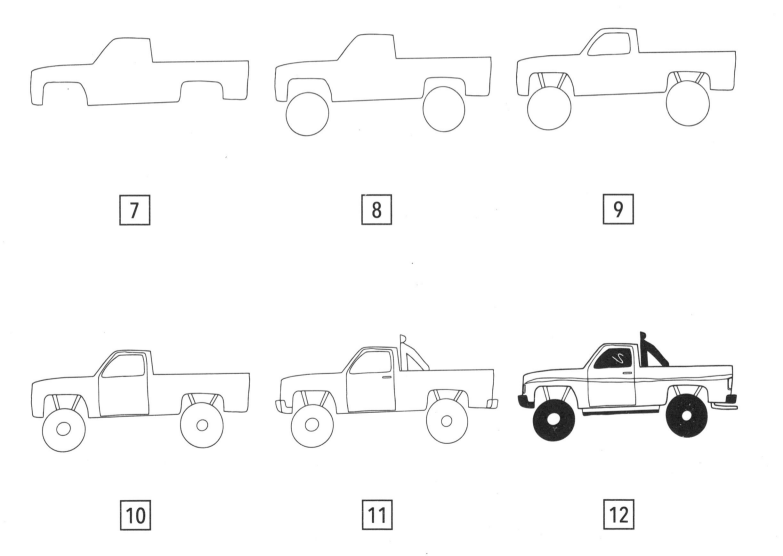

7

8

9

10

11

12

31

CAR

There are more cars than people in the world.

1

2

3

4

5

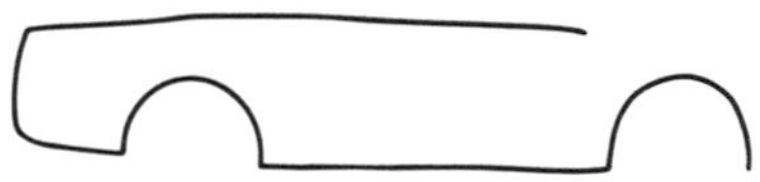

6

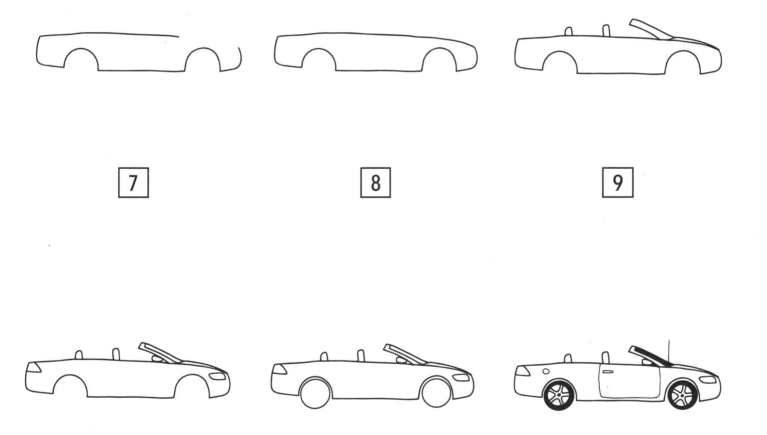

7

8

9

10

11

12

SAILBOAT

The right side of a sailboat is called the starboard. The left side is called the port.

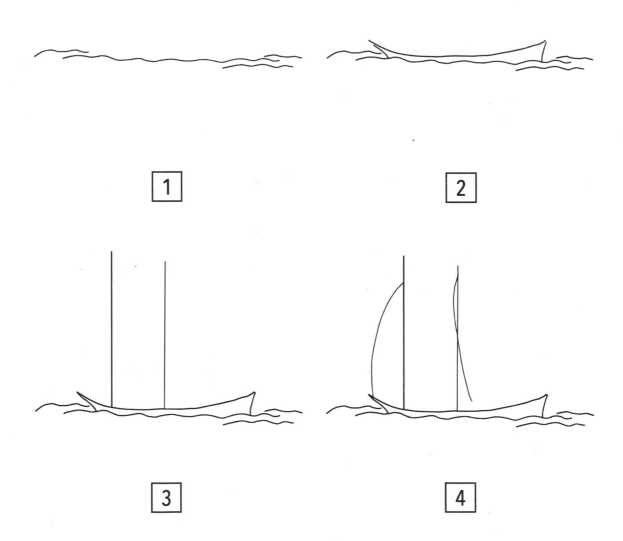

1

2

3

4

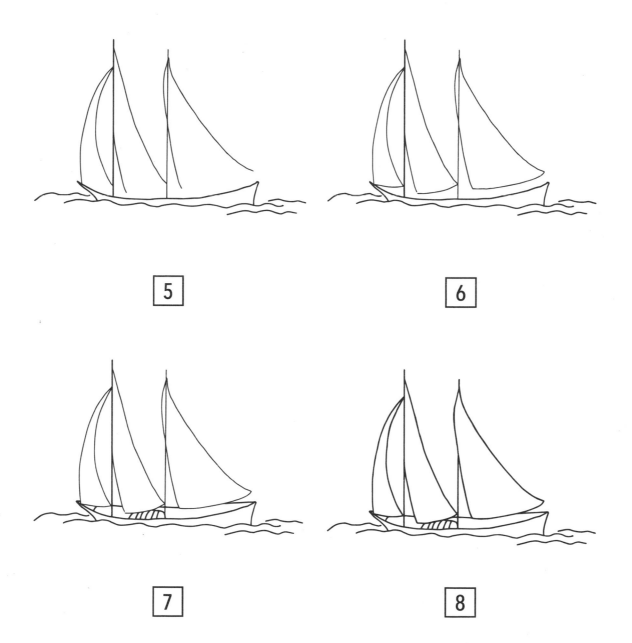

5

6

7

8

OCEAN

Around 71% of the Earth's surface is covered by oceans.

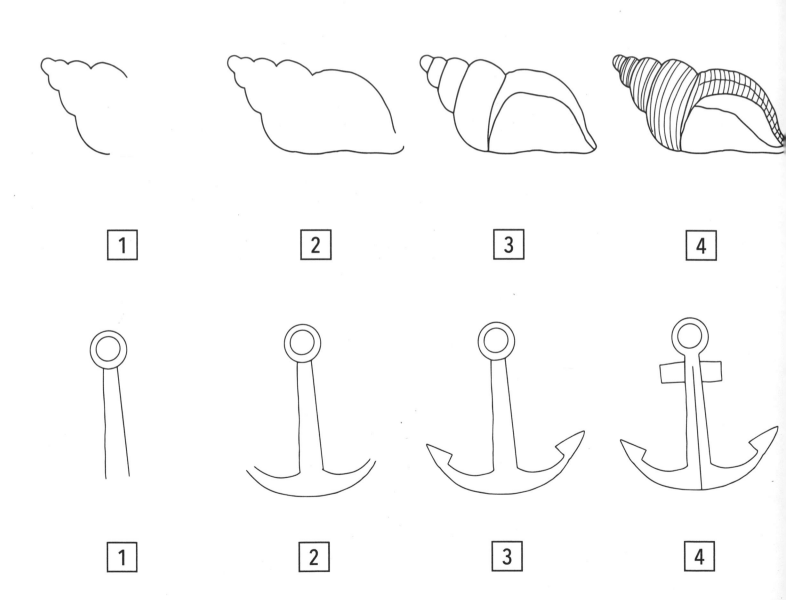

1

2

3

4

1

2

3

4

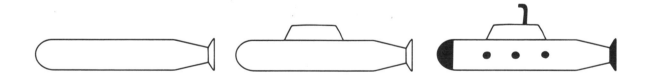

1

2

3

4

5

6

SPACE

A spacecraft has been sent to every planet in our solar system.

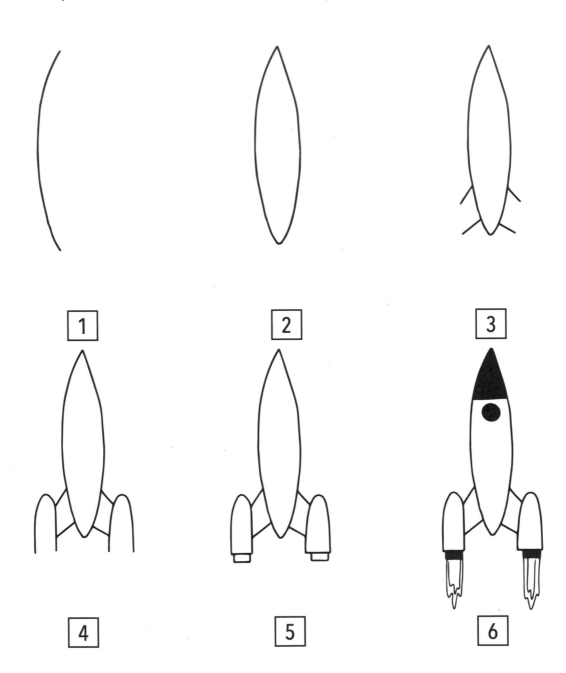

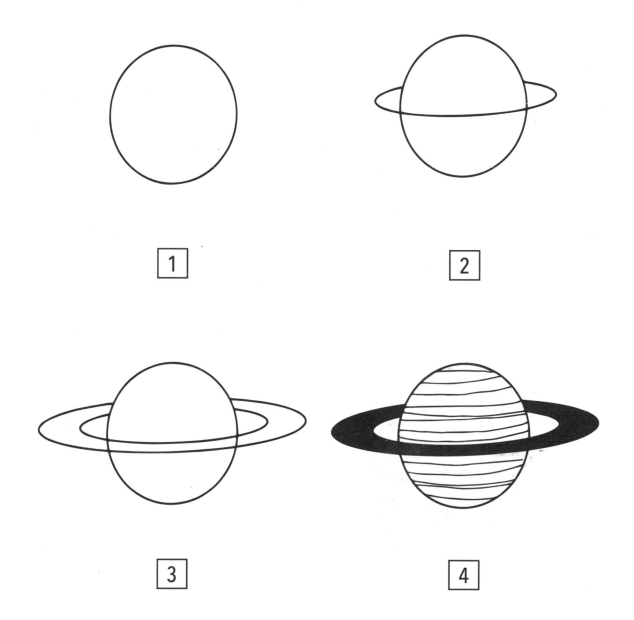

1

2

3

4

HOT AIR BALLOON

The balloon shape on top is actually called the envelope.

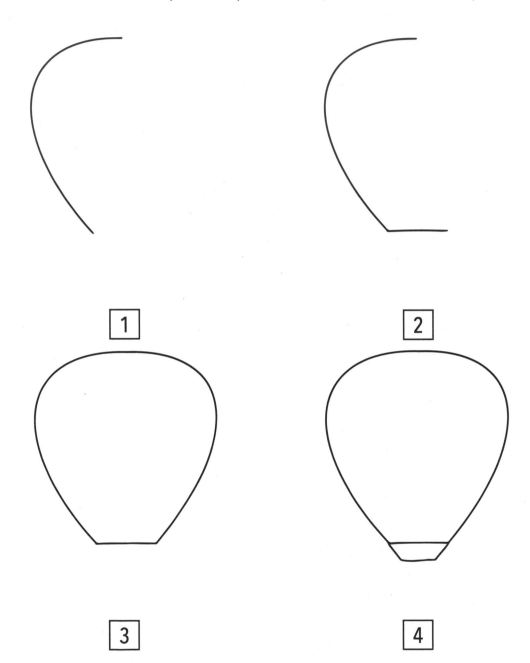

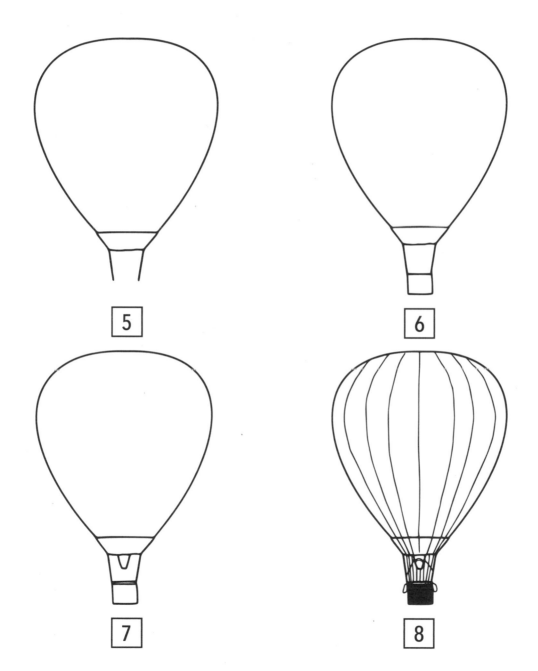

5

6

7

8

CASTLE

Castles used to be built without any toilets. Instead they just had holes in the ground.

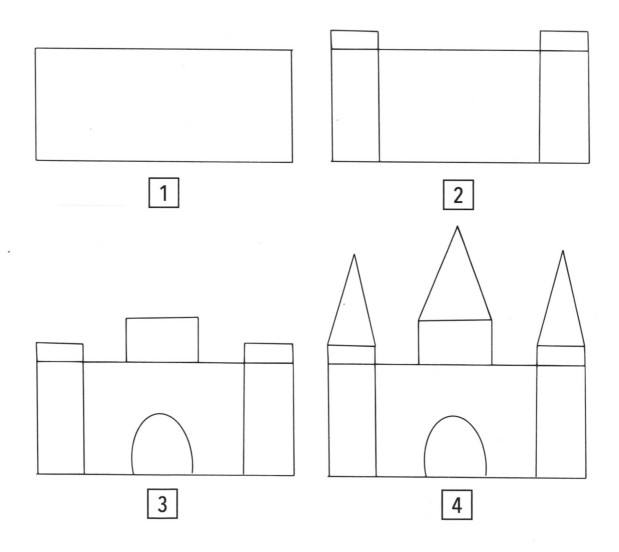

5

6

7

8

AIRPLANE

The weather outside can affect a paper airplane being thrown indoors.

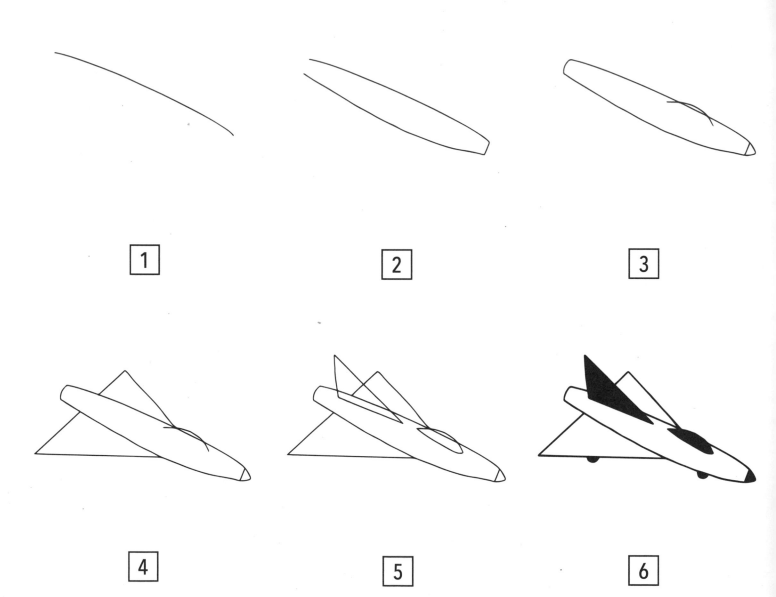

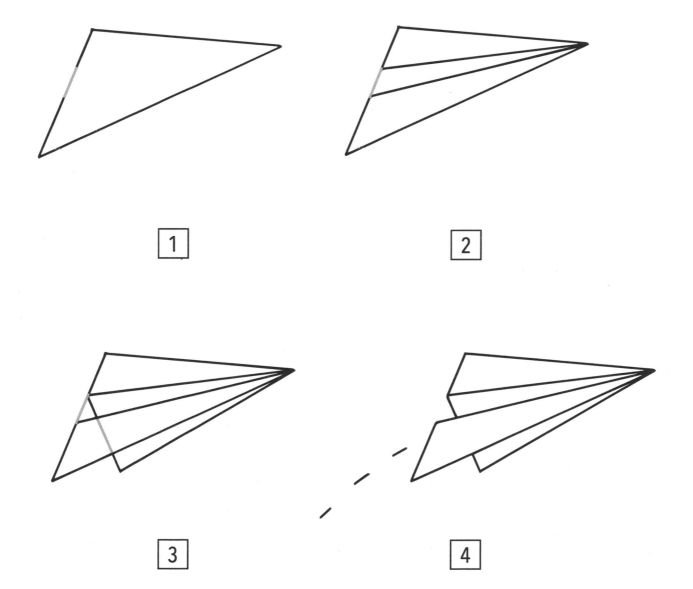

1

2

3

4

UNICORN

A magical animal that looks a lot like a horse.

1

2

3

4

5

6

7

8

9

10

11

12

ASTRONAUT

Neil Armstrong was the first man to walk on the moon.

1

2

3

4

5

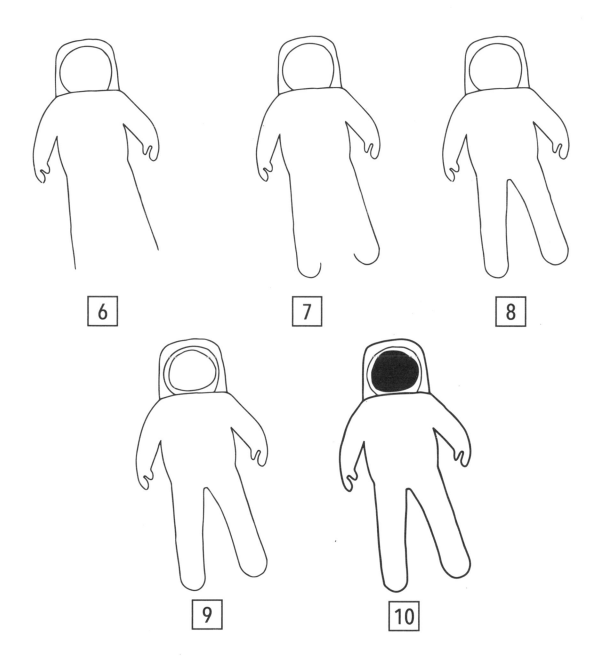

6

7

8

9

10

DRAGON

Since dragons are a make-believe animal, they can have many different looks and powers.

1

2

3

4

5

6

7

8

9

10

PEACE HAND

The peace sign is also known as the V-sign, which first started as a symbol for victory.

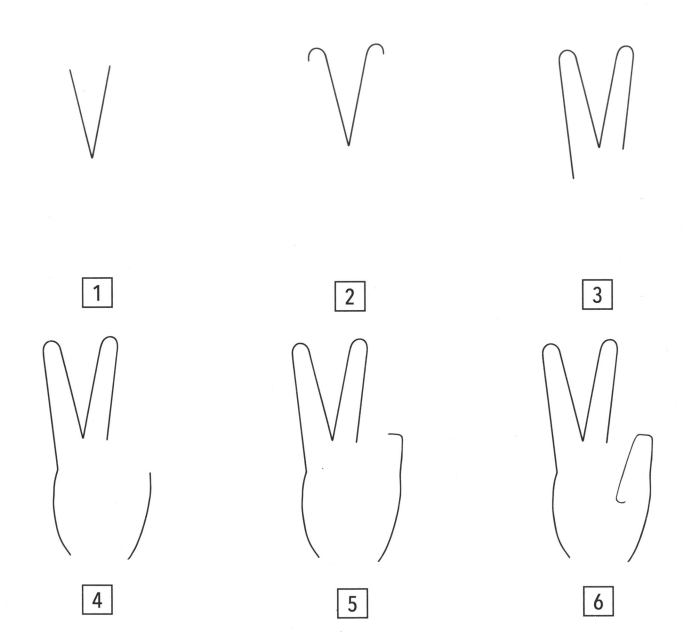

1

2

3

4

5

6

7

8

9

10

11

12

CACTUS

Two or more cactus are called cacti.

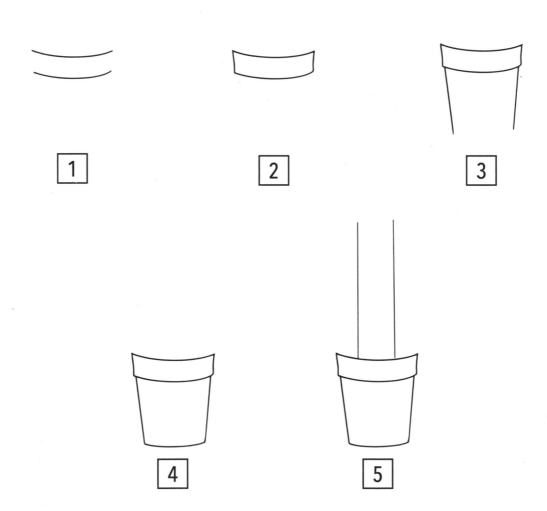

1

2

3

4

5

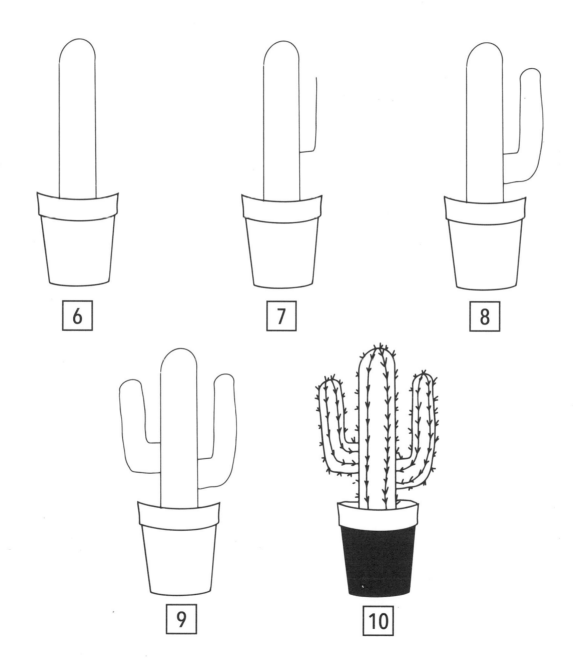

6

7

8

9

10

FLOWER

There are thousands of different kinds of flowers, with no two flowers exactly the same.

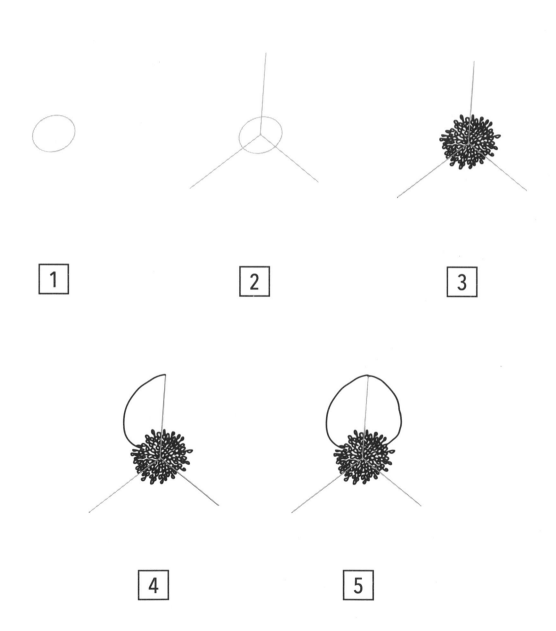

1

2

3

4

5

6

7

8

9

10

CAT

Alli has two cats. This is a drawing of her cat Emmie.

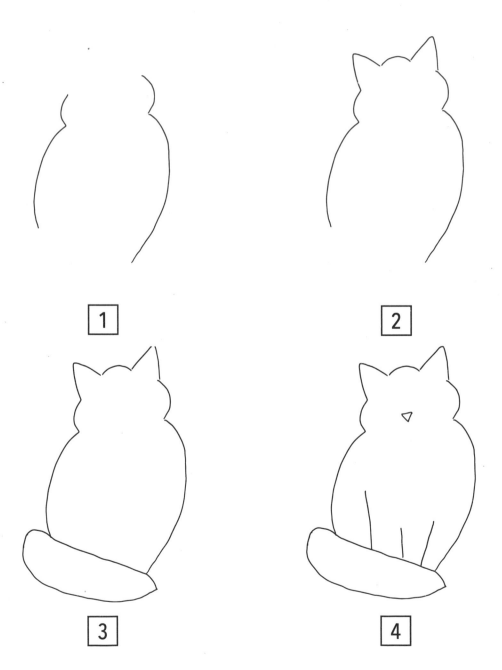

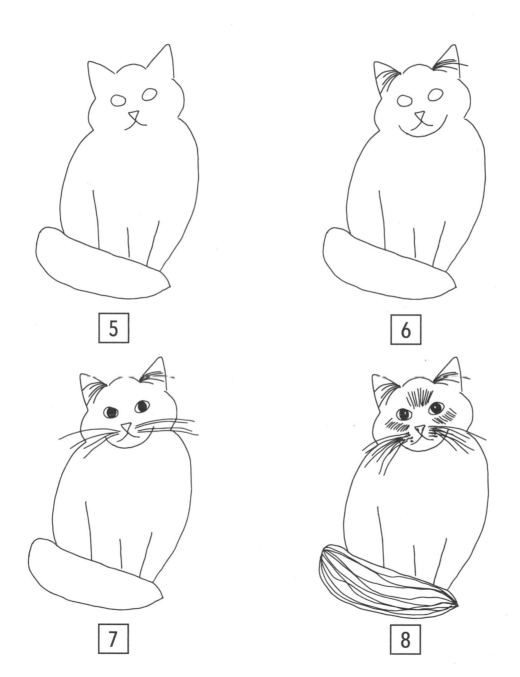

5

6

7

8

DOG

There are over 300 different kinds of dog breeds. This is a drawing of a French bulldog.

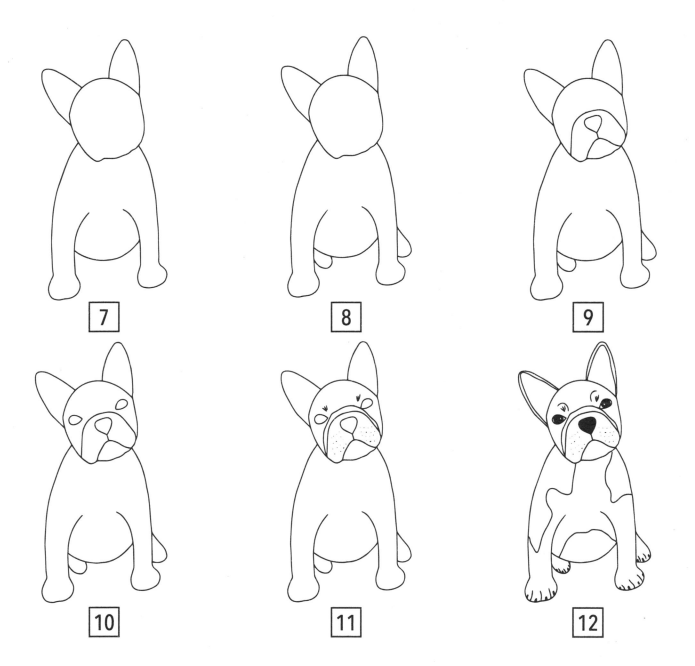

7

8

9

10

11

12

HEDGEHOG

Hedgehogs have over 5,000 spines (known as quills) on their backs!
Don't worry, you don't have to draw them all!

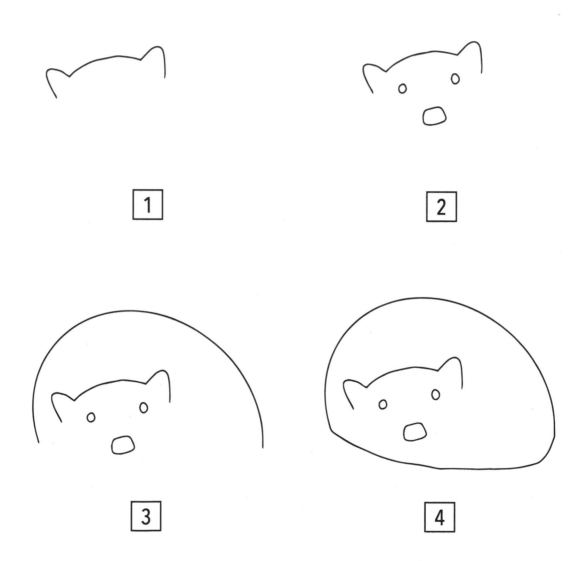

1

2

3

4

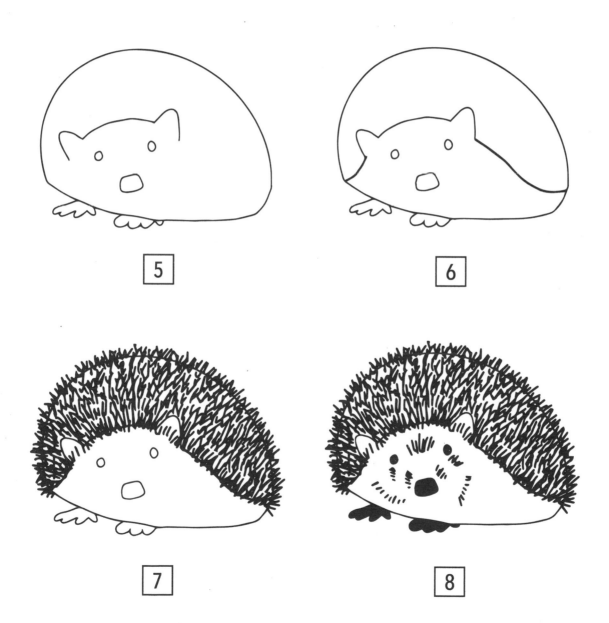

5

6

7

8

BUTTERFLY

Butterflies grow their wings inside a cocoon for an average of 30 days.

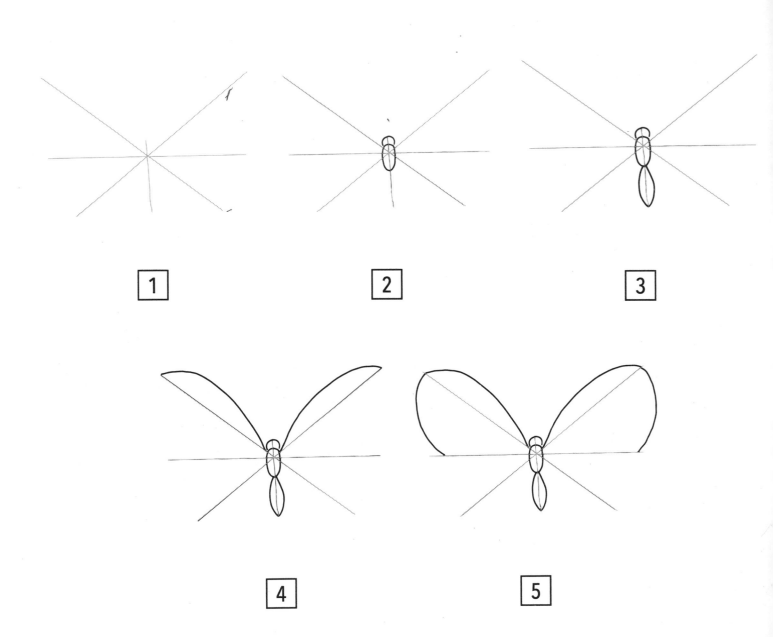

1

2

3

4

5

6

7

8

9

10

BEETLE

Beetles are the largest group of species, with over 350,000 different kinds.

1

2

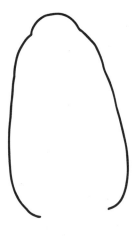

3

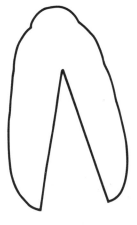

4

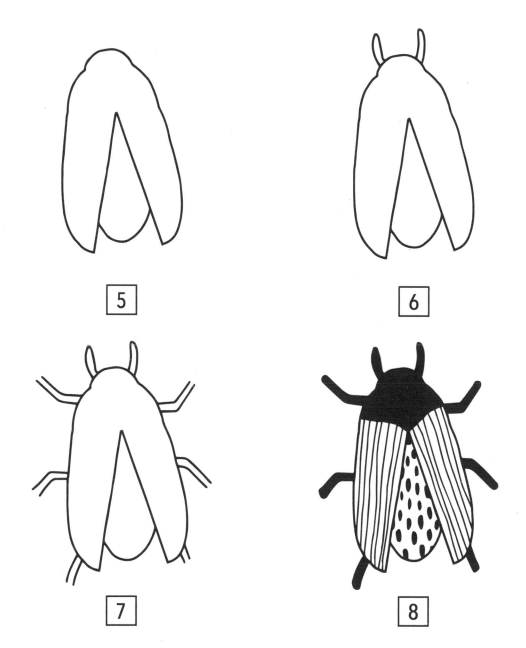

5

6

7

8

LIZARD

Lizards use their tongues to smell.

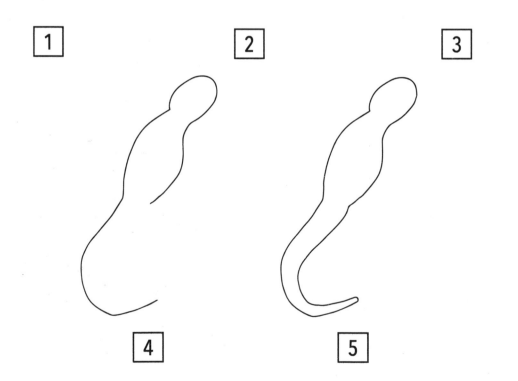

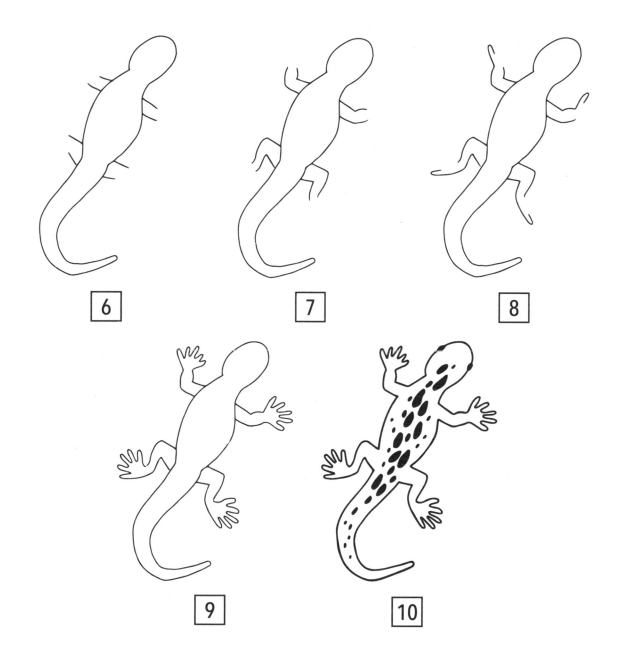

6

7

8

9

10

PENGUIN

Penguins spend up to 75% of their lives in water.

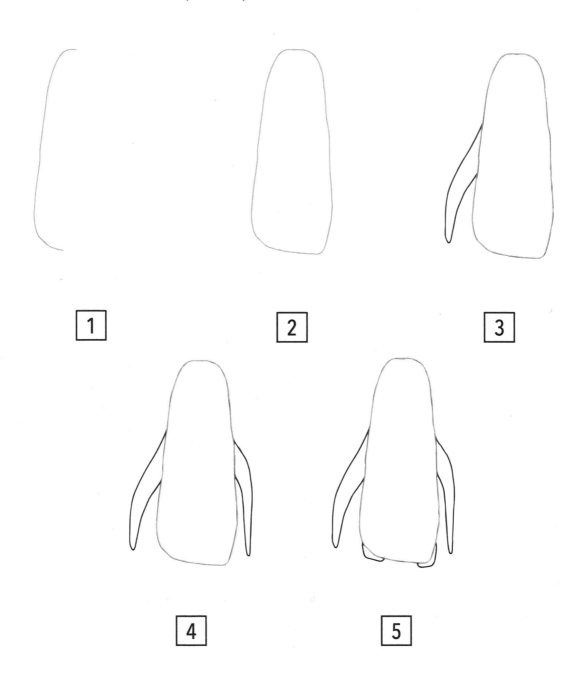

1

2

3

4

5

6

7

8

9

10

WHALE

The marks on the Humpback whale are unique to each whale, like a fingerprint!

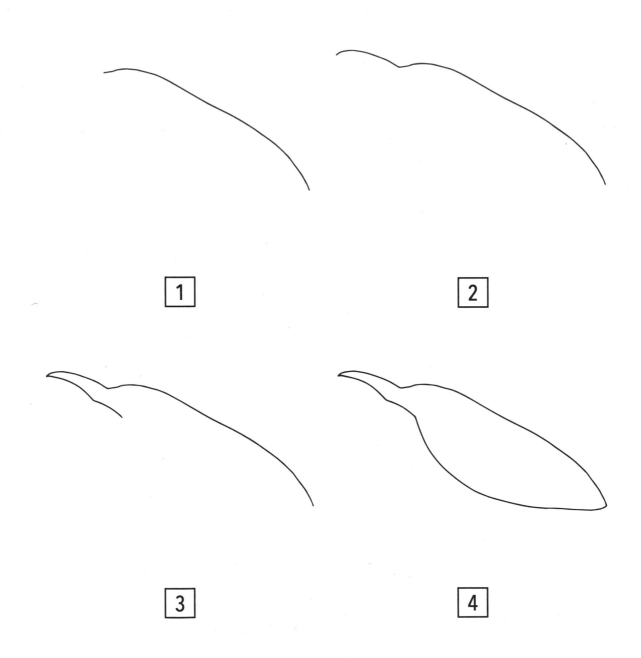

1

2

3

4

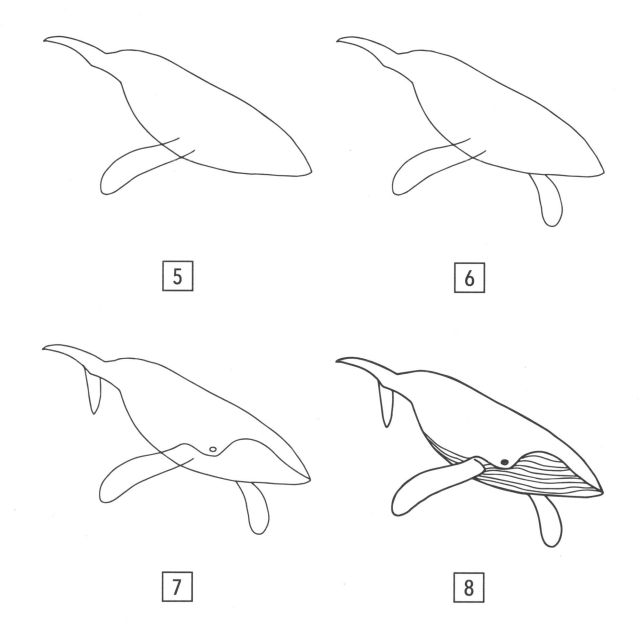

5

6

7

8

TURTLE

Female sea turtles lay their eggs at the same location they were born.

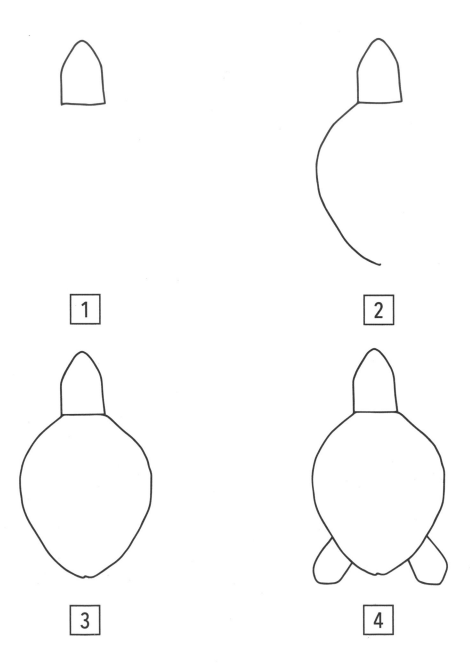

5

6

7

8

About Alli K

NAME: Alli Koch

HOME: Dallas, Texas

BIRTHDAY: March 20, 1991

FAVORITE COLOR: Black

FAVORITE FOOD: Waffle fries and a large sweet tea

JOB: I am a full-time artist! I sell my art online, paint on the side of buildings, and teach others how to draw or be creative

FAVORITE THING: my planner or blanket

PETS: I have two cats, Emmie and Cleo

CAR: Jeep

FAMILY: Married to my high school sweetheart

FAVORITE MOVIE: Cinderella, from 2015

FAVORITE TO DO: Naps, or having lunch with my friends